ARUNDEL CASTLE

A GUIDE

CONTENTS

Published by Arundel Castle Trustees Ltd, Arundel Castle, West Sussex BN18 9AB
Tel: 01903 882173 www.arundelcastle.org
Written by John Martin Robinson
Photographs by Paul Barker
except for: Leigh Simpson – page 39 (top right and bottom);
Mark Fiennes – pages 32, 35 & 40
Portrait of *Henry Howard, the 'Poet' Earl of Surrey* on
pages 24 & 52 courtesy of National Portrait Gallery
Drawings on pages 5 & 14 by Graham Butler
Garden plan on page 48 by Neil Gower
Front cover photograph by Skyscan

Opposite: Thomas, 3rd Duke of Norfolk

ISBN 978-1-86077-612-0

DESIGNED BY LIBANUS PRESS LTD, MARLBOROUGH
PRINTED BY HAMPTON PRINTING (BRISTOL) LTD

INTRODUCTION

Arundel Castle is a well preserved Norman Castle with a Keep, Gatehouse, Barbican and curtain wall, combined with a very large Victorian country house. The latter is one of the masterpieces of the 19th-century Gothic Revival with magnificent state rooms, while the former has the same 'figure of 8' plan as (the slightly later) Windsor Castle, with a central motte (artificial earth mound) supporting a stone shell keep, flanked by two outer baileys (defensive walled courtyards). The South Bailey or Quadrangle contains the main residential accommodation, and has done since the 12th century, while the North Bailey has always been a private garden.

The castle was founded on Christmas Day 1067 when William the Conqueror, having successfully invaded England and won the throne, held his first Christmas Court at Gloucester. There he rewarded his trusted supporters with large estates on condition that they built defensive castles. A third of Sussex was granted by William I to his kinsman Roger de Montgomery who had been left behind to look after Normandy during the Battle of Hastings. The new castle at Arundel was one of a chain of defensive fortresses along the south coast erected by William's followers as a deterrent to future cross-Channel invasions, with the royal castles of Dover in Kent and Carisbrooke on the Isle of Wight on either flank. Several of these castles like Lewes and Bramber originally had a similar plan to Arundel with two baileys and greater and lesser mottes and a gatehouse tower.

Arundel was a naturally defensive site, four miles from the sea, protecting the Arun Gap where the river flows through the South Downs. A Saxon earthwork survives on the opposite bank at Warningcamp, and there may have been something similar at Arundel too. Roger de Montgomery immediately began construction of an ambitious earth and timber fortification in 1068, creating large defensive ditches and banks on the landward side, erecting a great motte almost 100 feet (30 metres) high and a lesser motte at the North end, as well as enclosing the baileys with timber fences. These initial defences were gradually strengthened and replaced with masonry, beginning with the gatehouse tower built of Pulborough stone, which dates from *circa* 1070. In the course of the next hundred years all the curtain wall round both baileys was rebuilt, largely in Sussex flintwork; most of which still survives. The battlements and turrets were restored in the 19th century but the majority of the walls are original.

Roger de Montgomery's son, Robert, rebelled against King Henry I and was exiled as a result; his lands and Arundel Castle being taken back by the Crown. They remained in royal hands until 1138. In that year Arundel was granted as her

Queen Adeliza of Louvain

dower to Queen Adeliza of Louvain, the widow of Henry I who died in 1135. She married as her second husband William d'Aubigny (de Albini) of Buckenham in Norfolk, who was created Earl of Sussex. Contemporary chronicles describe William as 'puffed up' with pride at his grand royal marriage. He was certainly a great castle-builder and was responsible for a splendid shell keep at New Buckenham, his family property in Norfolk, as well as the ornate square keep at Castle Rising near Kings Lynn which was also part of Adeliza's dower. At Arundel he replaced the original timber tower on the motte with an ambitious masonry keep proclaiming his lordly status. Whereas the earlier walls and towers had all been of local Sussex materials, William de Albini's shell keep was of finest ashlar stone, brought across the Channel by barge from Caen in Normandy.

After Adeliza's and William de Albini's deaths, Arundel, as Adeliza's dower, reverted to the Crown. While in royal hands Henry II built a new residential range in the South Bailey. However he recognised the claim of William's son and returned the Castle to him. It was thereafter treated as a non-royal hereditary property.

William de Albini's Keep had contained his own residence, but later in the Middle Ages his successors through the female line, the Fitzalan Earls of Arundel, who succeeded in 1243, built a more convenient quadrangular house with a Great Hall and separate lodgings or apartments round the South Bailey, incorporating Henry II's South Range. Part of the shell of this underlies the present Victorian house there. The Fitzalans, notably the very rich 3rd and 4th Earls, carried out extensive building works in the later 14th century. They added the Barbican to the outside of the Gatehouse, and this survives as the best-preserved part of the medieval buildings, as does the Beaumont or Bevis Tower which they added to the North Bailey at the same date.

There were twelve Fitzalan Earls of Arundel, but

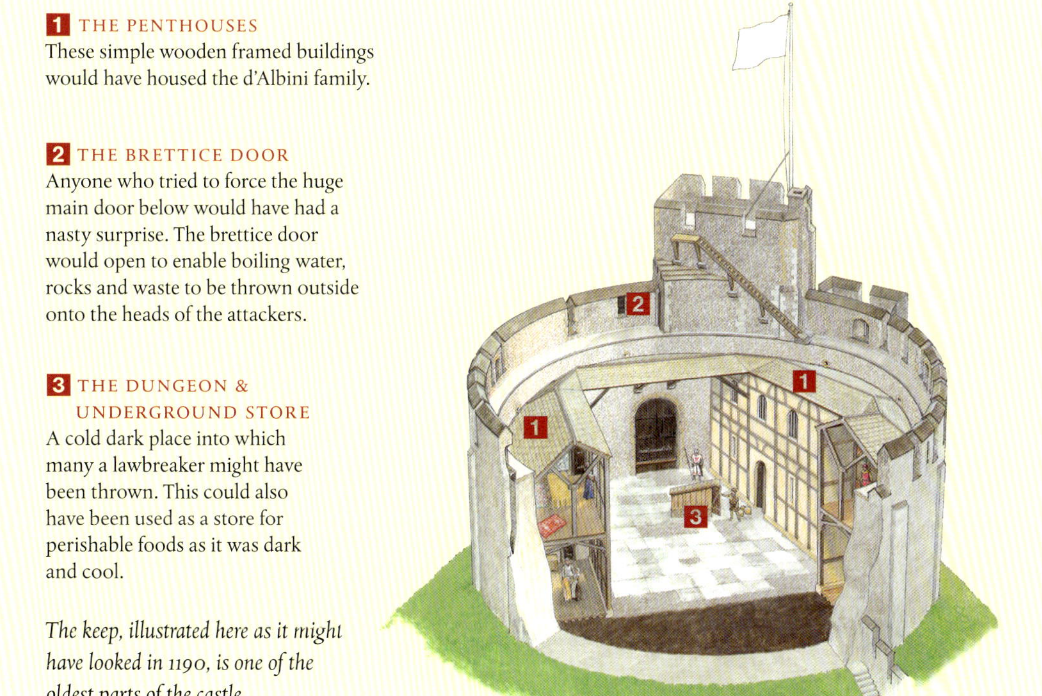

The keep, illustrated here as it might have looked in 1190, is one of the oldest parts of the castle.

the son of the last Earl died young and on the 12th Earl's own death in 1580 the Castle was inherited by his grandson Philip Howard whose mother, Lady Mary Fitzalan, had married the 4th Duke of Norfolk. Arundel has belonged to the Howards, Earls of Arundel and Dukes of Norfolk ever since. But they owned several houses of their own in Norfolk and Surrey in the 16th and 17th centuries and in Nottinghamshire in the 18th century, so only visited the Castle occasionally.

During the English Civil War the Castle was besieged in 1644 by the Parliamentarians under General Waller who captured and subsequently 'slighted' or part-demolished it to prevent it being defended again. Most of the west side of the South Bailey was demolished, including the Fitzalans' Great Hall and the south-west section of the Norman curtain wall. It was only in 1708 that the 8th Duke of Norfolk patched up the South Range as an occasional residence, with a plain red brick Georgian front to the Quadrangle as if it were in a town square. He and his successors lived mainly at Worksop Manor in Nottinghamshire (sold in 1838) and Norfolk House in London (sold in 1938), and only stayed at Arundel for about a fortnight each year to supervise estate business.

Towards the end of the 18th century, however, the 11th Duke of Norfolk, inspired by the dawning Romantic Movement and the revival of interest in the Gothic and the Middle Ages, decided to make the castle the principal ducal seat, at the same time that George III began the restoration of Windsor. He reconstructed the South, East and West Ranges of the Lower Bailey to his own design – a hybrid of Norman and Perpendicular – in stages between 1789 and his death in 1815 when he left parts of the new house unfinished. His amateur efforts were not admired by either his successors or by visitors; Queen Victoria described it in her 'Journal' as 'bad architecture'! The criticism was taken to heart, and after he inherited, Henry, 15th Duke of Norfolk carried out a massive and scholarly reconstruction of the whole house (except for the library) between 1875 and 1900, as well as carefully restoring the remains of the Norman Castle. His project included new roads, a new water supply and *electric* light, and cost over half a million pounds in the money of the day, of which the Victorian electric light alone came to the huge sum of £35,000.

Duke Henry chose as his architect Charles Alban Buckler. He was the third generation of an antiquarian architectural dynasty based in Oxford where they restored many of the Colleges and whose work spanned the 19th century. His grandfather John Buckler was Surveyor to Magdalen College; his father John Chessell Buckler is famous for his water colours of medieval cathedrals and manor houses; Charles Alban Buckler himself was primarily a church architect, as well as being a Catholic convert, and Surrey Herald Extraordinary. Arundel Castle is his largest and most important commission. Like many Victorian buildings, St Pancras Station for instance, it combined progressive industrial technology with historically inspired architecture. It had concrete foundations, coal-fired central heating, a Merryweather fire-fighting system (with steam-powered engine), a modern pumped water supply with bathrooms, 65 water-closets, and an hydraulic lift; it was one of the first houses in England to have electric light, installed from 1892 with its own steam turbine generator. The scholarly Gothic architecture, on the other hand, was inspired entirely by English and French examples of the mid-13th century including Westminster Abbey, Winchester Castle, Le Mans Cathedral, and the studies of Pugin in England and Viollet le Duc in France. The craftsmanship, much of it executed by Rattee & Kett of Cambridge, with stained glass and metal work by Hardman of Birmingham (firms which still exist), is of superb quality. The exterior of the house is faced in Doulting stone from Somerset, while the interior is of fine Cotswold stone from Painswick in Gloucestershire. The window frames are not iron

The West Front

but all of gun metal (a tough bronze alloy, which does not need painting and does not expand in heat). It was a magnificent job.

Such was the excellence of the Victorian work that Arundel survived through the first three quarters of the 20th century with little structural maintenance. During the Second World War it played a role as part of the south coast defences (a role not forseen by the 15th Duke or his architect Buckler when they perfected the medieval fortifications), and was occupied by British, American and Commonwealth troops up to the D-Day landings in 1944.

After the War the house was re-opened to the public in 1947, continuing a tradition dating back to the 18th century. (The 2nd edition of the Guide Book was printed in 1818.) Whereas before the War the income from visitors was given to charity, since then it has made a valued contribution to the maintenance of the building itself.

In 1962 the castle ceased to be lived in on a regular basis when Bernard, 16th Duke, built a new house in the park as a private residence, which was subsequently occupied by his widow. When Duke Bernard in turn was succeeded by his cousin Miles as 17th Duke in 1975, however, a new era began. The structure of the castle, including all the Norman and medieval fortifications and the Fitzalan Chapel was thoroughly restored, mainly by the architects Seely & Paget, and a charitable trust was established for the future preservation of the fabric, and to which the principal contents were lent on a long-term agreement. This was the first arrangement of this type to preserve an historic house, and it has since been copied by many of the most important houses in England and Scotland.

The present 18th Duke of Norfolk, prior to succeeding to the dukedom and following his marriage in 1987 took the decision to move back into the Castle and make it once more the family home. Over the last twenty years he and his wife Georgina, with the Castle Trustees, have restored and redecorated the whole interior to its Victorian magnificence, as well as improving the visitor facilities. The Duchess is also personally responsible for all the present gardens, created on a scale and with a character to match the historic architecture. The Duke has restored the park (following the great storm in 1987 which blew down 90% of the old trees and wrecked the boundary walls) and has initiated a conservation plan to plant new hedges and conserve the wildlife in the surrounding estate which stretches for miles over the beautiful downland. The park is open freely every day, and the agricultural land beyond can be explored by a network of footpaths or along the banks of the River Arun (the bed of which belongs to the Estate as far as Pulborough). It is partly thanks to the Norfolk Estate and its land-owning neighbours in Sussex that this rural area of chalk downs and river valleys has survived the intense industrialisation and urbanisation of the last two centuries, despite its close proximity to London and the Coast. The Castle now contains and displays nearly all the family's art collections and historic archives, brought from several other houses including Worksop and Norfolk House, in a building which has passed largely by descent since 1138 and which embodies much of English history.

18th-century painting of The Keep and Quadrangle by James Canter

THE CASTLE

THE CASTLE

The first impression of the South Front seen from the winding drive leading up from the Lower Lodge is of Victorian work of the 1870s and 1880s by C. A. Buckler, especially the prominent gabled and turreted dining room projection and the two massive circular towers and kitchen block at the west end. The South Front, however, incorporates substantial fabric dating from the 12th century, including two late Norman windows now blocked, and projecting buttresses of the same date.

On the west side the curtain wall can be seen, its external flintwork refaced in the 19th century and in 1976, as far as the Barbican which is approached by a wooden drawbridge over the impressively deep dry moat or ditch. This continues round the foot of the motte and along the west and north sides of the North Bailey. The motte and ditch are part of Roger de Montgomery's original earthworks of 1068. The drawbridge is the best place to appreciate the Norman and medieval Castle; the impressive height of the motte, the early 12th-century Keep, the late 14th-century Barbican with two square towers flanking the entrance gate through which can be seen the original Norman archways, *circa* 1070. On the far side of the keep can be seen the late 14th-century Bevis Tower with angular buttresses and shouldered Caernarvon arches to the windows like those in the Barbican. The curtain wall round the North Bailey with three projecting towers is

South aspect – blocked window in the Henry II range built around 1180

The Gatehouse Tower – The Officer's Room

largely 12th-century, built of flint with Pulborough stone dressings. It is similar to Framlingham Castle in Suffolk. It was repaired in the 16th century and again in the 19th when the wallwalk, battlements and turrets were all replaced by Buckler combining the evidence of some surviving bits with a certain degree of romantic imagination.

The Keep and other original parts are approached via a staircase from the Stone Hall. A narrow passage along the top of the south-west curtain wall, (which gives an idea of the thickness of these outer masonry fortifications) leads to the Gatehouse.

THE GATEHOUSE TOWER

The Gatehouse Tower is, apart from the earthworks, the oldest part of the castle, built *circa* 1070 of Pulborough stone with the upper storeys of Sussex flintwork. It is four storeys high with two taller turrets on the outside face containing spiral staircases. The original entrance archway has a well-preserved portcullis groove identical to that at Arques-la-Bataille near Dieppe, a contemporary castle in Normandy. The existing portcullis and machinery is an accurate Victorian re-creation, and gives a good idea of how the medieval one worked.

Many of the towers and subsidiary parts of the castle were occupied as individual lodgings for officials and senior servants in the medieval and Tudor periods. Some of these were 'bedsits' and some 'flats' with several rooms. The Gatehouse was the residence of the Constable of the Castle, the senior official under the Fitzalan Earls of Arundel. The first-floor apartment was his principal room. Since the 18th century it has been known as 'Queen Matilda's Room' after the Queen-Empress, daughter of Henry I, who *may* have stayed here with her step-mother Adeliza of Louvain. The two-arched Norman window is an original feature. The square fireplace, with its Tudor brick lining, is 16th-century. In the second floor room, the fireplace again is 16th-century. The upper floor is a bedroom; it was thoroughly repaired, including the window, in the 19th century. The oak furniture was collected by the 15th Duke and includes a four-poster bed. The stone cannon balls are English 17th-century

The Gatehouse Tower – portcullis machinery

and survive from the Civil War siege. At the top of the gatehouse, not open to the public, is a fine 18th-century clock mechanism. This has no outer face or dial but strikes the hours and the quarters.

THE BARBICAN

This is one of the major surviving additions of the Fitzalan Earls of Arundel. It dates from the late 14th century and was part of a general Perpendicular overhaul of Arundel, including the Fitzalan Chapel, begun by Richard the 3rd Earl (who had inherited a large fortune from his mother Alice de Warenne) and his son the 4th Earl. It has a distinctive plan with an open court between the old Gatehouse and the Barbican proper, and a pair of square towers flanking the entrance, similar to the contemporary Barbican at Warwick Castle. The first floor, over the archway, comprises an independent apartment with a central hall and two tower rooms and two closets. The hall ceiling has the original moulded timber roof beams. The Barbican is built of flint with Pulborough stone dressings and Caernarvon arched windows. It retains its original battlements and chimneys.

THE CURTAIN WALL

The wall-walk leading up the side of the Motte from the Gatehouse to the Keep is partly contemporary

The Keep and Well Tower

The Fitzalan Horse

The Howard Lion

The Barbican and Gatehouse

The Bevis Tower

with the Gatehouse itself. The lower part incorporates squared blocks of Pulborough stone, although the upper parts are of flint. This was the first part of the encircling wall to be rebuilt in solid masonry and dates from the late 11th century. The battlements were reinstated *circa* 1900 on the evidence of originals surviving on the Keep.

THE KEEP

The Keep is an open shell of oval plan, 59 feet by 67 feet and 30 feet high (19 by 22 by 9 metres). It was built of Caen stone by William de Albini, shortly after his marriage to Adeliza of Louvain in 1138, on top of the original post-Conquest motte. It has no windows to the outside but to the south is a large Norman doorway, now blocked, boldly decorated with zigzag and scroll mouldings, a rare feature in this position. The walls are punctuated by flat buttresses and terminate in battlements. When first built it contained the best residential accommodation lit from an inner court. Though it is now open to the sky, some of the late 14th-century fireplaces survive and under the floor in the centre is a store room for provisions in case of a siege.

A staircase gives access to the wall-walk from which there are magnificent views towards the coast on the south, the town and Cathedral on the west, the Park on the north and along the river to the Arun Gap on the east.

The Keep was carefully restored for the 15th Duke by John Morley of Cambridge in 1900–06 and again in 1976–78 by Seely and Paget. John Morley also designed the Bevis Gateway and Bridge on the north side of the Motte. A standard is always flown from the top of the Well Tower when the Duke of Norfolk is in residence.

THE FORE-BUILDING

The Fore-building, protecting the entrance to the Keep was added in the late 12th century when William de Albini's large original doorway on the south side of the Keep was blocked, no doubt at the time there was a permanent move to the new house in the bailey below.

THE WELL TOWER AND ST MARTIN'S TOWER

The Well Tower and St Martin's Tower were both added at the same time to enhance the defensive character of the Keep. The well is over 100 feet (31 metres) deep, and goes right down through the motte to the water table below. It provided the Keep, the Castle's main strong point, with its own independent water supply in case of a prolonged siege.

The upper part of St Martin's Tower contained a little chapel dedicated to St Martin of Tours, patron saint of soldiers. Both the Montgomery and the de Albini families had a special devotion to St Martin. This little oratory was superseded by a larger castle chapel in the South Bailey in the Middle Ages (now the dining room). The two-arched window is another original Norman survival. It gives a good view of the quadrangle.

1 ST MARTIN'S CHAPEL
2 THE PORTCULLIS
3 THE GUARD ROOM
4 THE WELL

The Keep around 1190 AD

THE HOUSE

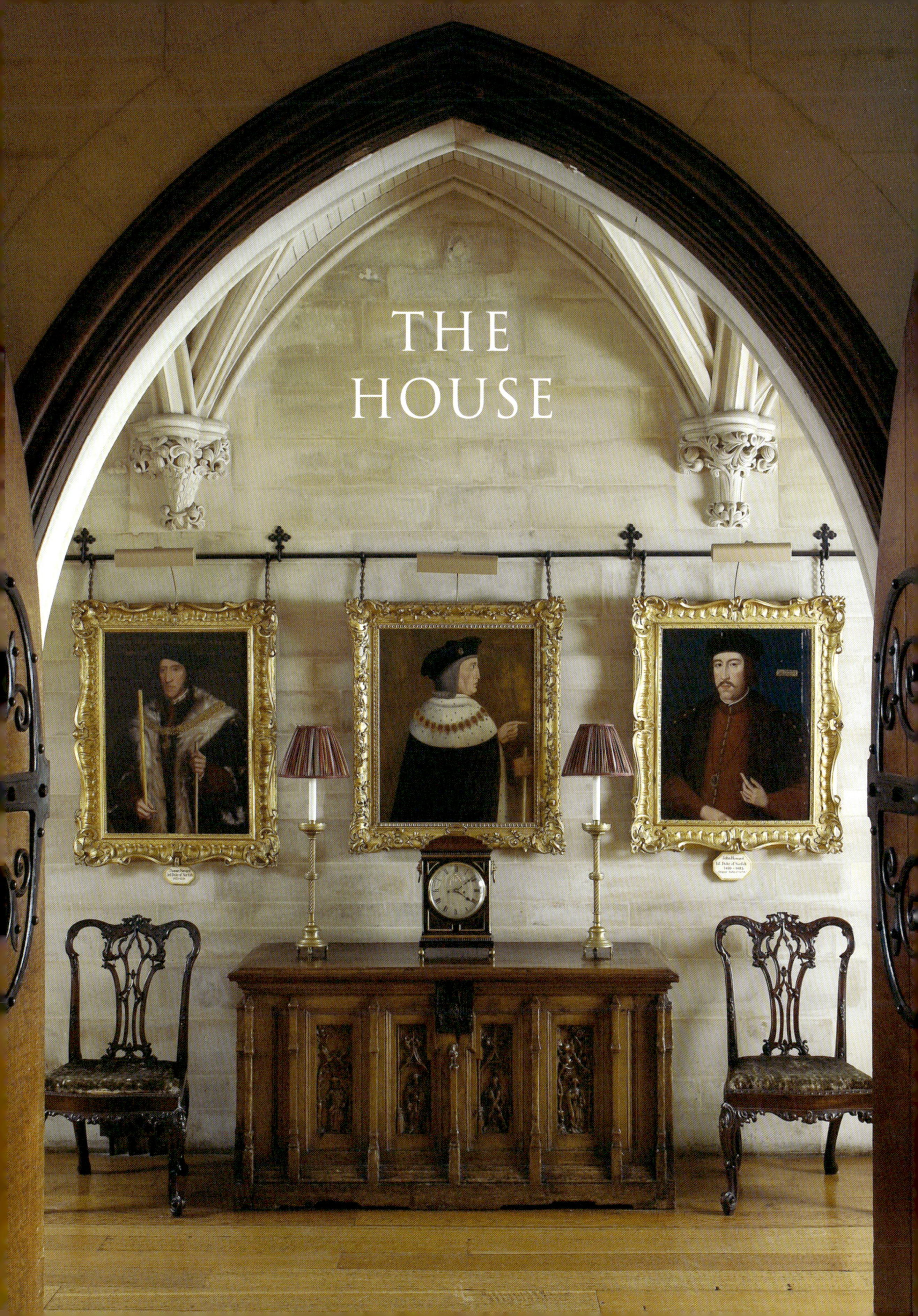

VISITOR ENTRANCE

The visitor entrance is on the west side. The 1875 archway is based on a medieval original at Glastonbury Abbey.

THE STONE HALL AND STAIRS

The Stone Hall is a small stone-vaulted undercroft with slim circular columns down the centre. The Waiting Room, adjoining, is used as an exhibition space for a changing display of documents from the Duke of Norfolk's Archives, which are one of the most important private collections in England.

The 18th-century mahogany hall chairs and the Regency Regulator clock are from Norfolk House, the London house of the Dukes of Norfolk in St James's Square, demolished in 1938 when the contents were brought to Arundel. Lining the staircase are a number of 17th-century iron chests of German origin and some Italian early 17th-century walnut chairs. They form an introduction to the rare, cosmopolitan, even exotic, contents of the principal rooms, many of them collected by the 15th Duke in the 1880s and 1890s to complement the Gothic architecture.

The iron hinges of the double doors at the top, decorated with Fitzalan oak leaves, a reference to the Duke of Norfolk's coat of arms, are typical of the ironwork designed by Buckler. It is worth noting similar details of Victorian craftsmanship throughout the Castle: door hinges, curtain brackets, electric light fittings, fire dogs and even the original central heating radiators which are of polished gun metal.

THE ARMOURY

The collection of armour at Arundel is one of the few surviving Victorian assemblages of its kind. It was brought together largely by the 15th Duke of Norfolk in the 1880s with the assistance of the London dealer Charles Davis, and was acquired partly in France and partly from sales in London.

There are four suits of Maximilian-type armour which contain original 16th-century German pieces but were assembled in the 19th century to make complete figures as was then the fashion; there is also a coat of chain mail of early 16th-century date. On the corbels supporting the roof beams are four mid 17th-century Light Cavalry helmets from the English Civil War, and in the window bay, a heavy Flemish siege helmet *circa* 1610. The metal plated saddle dates from the 15th century and is a very rare survival.

The collection is notable for its 16th- to 18th-century pole arms, partizans, spears and glaives, many of them intended for ceremonial occasions rather than real warfare. They include a pair of partizans used at the Polish Coronation of Augustus the Strong of Saxony, a halberd made for the wedding of the Empress Maria Theresa of Austria in 1736, and a leading staff from the Court of the Gonzaga Dukes of Mantua.

The swords are also of special interest. The

The Armoury

oldest is 'Mongley', an English long sword dating from the 14th century, which has always been at Arundel and hangs in the window, as does a Chinese execution sword and a group of German 16th-century Processional swords. Some other early swords are displayed in a glass case, including a 15th-century Italian sword with gilt-etched blade and some English cup hilt rapiers *circa* 1610.

18th- and 19th-century family swords are arranged on boards in the alcove to the right of the entrance, and the circular wall trophy includes nine basket hilt 18th-century Scottish swords.

The octagonal centre table has a Florentine 16th-century top of Italian woods inlaid with ivory, made in the Grand Ducal workshops and incorporating the Medici Arms. The leather travelling trunk in the window bay belonged to Queen Catherine of Braganza, wife of Charles II, and was bequeathed to the Norfolk family by the last Catholic Earl of Shrewsbury in 1856. The Augsburg Cabinet with sycamore marquetry was made in 1550 for the Solis Sodeno family of Spain and bears their arms on the front.

THE CHAPEL

Dedicated to the Blessed Virgin Mary, the private chapel is the finest Victorian room in the Castle and one of the most perfect monuments of the 19th-century Catholic Revival in England. It was the last part of Buckler's rebuilding to be completed. The foundation stone was laid by the Archbishop of Southwark in 1894. It was commissioned by the 15th Duke in mid 13th-century style, drawing inspiration from examples like Lincoln Cathedral and Westminster Abbey. The floor and columns are of Purbeck marble (acquired when the medieval quarry in Dorset was briefly re-opened in the 1870s). The striped ceiling vault is of chalk and Painswick stone. Nearly every moulding and surface is richly carved. The Victorian craftsmanship here and throughout the Castle is of superb quality. The beautiful stained glass, inspired by that at Canterbury Cathedral, is by Hardman of Birmingham and depicts scenes from the life of Our Lady in deep, rich colours. The ceiling bosses also have scenes from the life of the Virgin. Hardman provided the metalwork including the gilt tabernacle inlaid with rock crystal, and the wrought iron electroliers.

Among the treasures displayed in the chapel are the silver altar vases made for the 8th Duke by Charles Kandler in 1730 and the two rare sets of early 18th-century English silver candlesticks on the side altars. The paintings include a Flemish triptych of the Adoration of the Magi by Pieter Coecke Van Aelst and a panel of the Garden of Gethsemane from the circle of the Master of Delft. The marble bust of Pope Pius IX is by Pietro Tenerani. In a turret above the Chapel is a set of bells, made specially at the Whitechapel Bell Foundry, which are in ringing condition. The Chapel is used regularly, and there are sung Masses on particular Feasts of the Year, including the Immaculate Conception. All the present Duke's children were baptised here.

THE BARONS' HALL

The vast size of the Barons' Hall is all the more breathtaking after the low vaults of the Stone Hall and staircase. It is 133 feet (41 metres) long and 50 feet (16 metres) high. This magnificent late Victorian architectural achievement, on the site of the medieval hall, replaces the smaller octagonal hall built by the 11th Duke in 1806–12 to commemorate the signing of Magna Carta, and dedicated to 'Liberty, asserted by the Barons in the reign of John', hence its name. The hammer-beam roof of oak from the estate was inspired by that at Penshurst and in the Guesten Hall at Worcester. The stained glass, as in the chapel, is by Hardman. Here it represents the history of the Fitzalan Howard family from the 12th to the 19th centuries by means of heraldry in the east windows and historical vignettes in the west. The Hall was re-wired in 2001 and the Gothic wrought iron electroliers made by a local blacksmith date from then. The two tapestries, dated 1754, are part of the Gobelins set depicting 'Les Nouvelles Indes', after François Desportes, woven by Neilson. They were bought by the 9th Duchess directly from the factory in France for the Great Room at Norfolk House and cost £9 a yard. (Two other pieces hang on the Grand Staircase.) The furniture includes an important series of continental 16th-century tables, chests and cupboards. The gilt early 18th-century needlework-covered chairs came from Worksop Manor. The little green and gilt sleigh is 19th-century Dutch. The large rococo sleigh decorated with painted panels is German 18th-century. The 9th Duchess's Sedan chair was made by Samuel Vaughan (royal Sedan chair-maker *circa* 1750) and comes from the hall at Norfolk House. Several of the paintings hanging on the oak wainscot are of considerable interest: a Spanish or Flemish triptych of the Life of the Virgin, a large Nativity by Marco Palmezzano, Cardinal Edward Howard by Julian Storey, King Charles I by Van Dyck, 'The Earl of Surrey defending his allegiance to Richard III after the Battle of Bosworth' painted in 1797 by Mather Brown (an American artist who worked in England), Cardinal Newman by Millais and a pair of landscapes by Jacques d'Artois.

The needlework chairs – c.1720

Round the upper part of the hall hang a series of full length portraits of historical interest:

East (Quadrangle) Side

Duke of Grafton by J. B. Van Loo
6th Duke of Norfolk, after Lely
7th Duke of Norfolk by Simon Verelst
Lord Maltravers by Mytens
3rd Duke of Norfolk after Holbein by Mytens
Henry Frederick Earl of Arundel after Mytens

West (Fireplace) Side

Lord Howard of Effingham by Mytens
Unknown man in Garter Robes
Duke of Leeds by J. Kerseboom
King James II by Kneller
Queen Mary of Modena by Kneller
Cardinal Philip Howard by Andrea Casali

THE PICTURE GALLERY

The Gallery was added to the Castle *circa* 1708 by the 8th Duke. It was gothicised by the 11th Duke in 1795 and again remodelled by Buckler for the 15th Duke. Here hang portraits of the Dukes and Duchesses of Norfolk and some of the Earls of Arundel, arranged in chronological order beginning at the west end. These are chiefly interesting as one of the great historic groups of family portraits but they include several which are individually fine, such as the Lawrence of Charlotte Sophia, wife of the 13th Duke. The portrait of Anne Dacre (widow of Philip, 13th Earl of Arundel) was acquired in 2007. Some of the 15th Duke's purchases of continental furniture line the walls, including several Italian chests.

The pair of splendid gilt side tables flanking the drawing room door have tops of Sicilian jasper. They were originally at Worksop Manor. The English early 18th-century gilt chairs with needlework seats have always been at Arundel, and the set of crisply carved chairs with 'ribbon' backs at the west end are based on a plate in a third edition of Chippendale's *Director* (1762). The arches to the Grand Staircase are flanked by busts of Charles I (1636) and Charles Lewis, Count Palatine of the Rhine (1637) by François Dieussart which are of special interest for they were commissioned by the 14th Earl of Arundel, known as the 'Collector Earl'. The other marble busts are of the 13th Duke of Norfolk and his family by John Francis and date from the 1840s.

BILLIARD ROOM

The Marshal Room now used as the Billiard Room was added to the Castle by the 11th Duke of Norfolk *circa* 1790 and remodelled as part of C. A. Buckler's campaign for the 15th Duke in the 1880s. The name recalls The Duke of Norfolk's office as Earl Marshal of England. The oak gothic furniture, including benches and chairs, was originally made by Charles Nosotti for the Victorian Billiard room in the East Wing, but was brought here when this room was converted to the Castle's Billiard Room. The carpet runner was designed by David Mlinaric and made by Grosvenor Woodward of Kidderminster. The large wrought iron light fitting is the most impressive of the original Buckler-designed 'electroliers' in the Castle.

THE DINING ROOM

This occupies the shell of the medieval chapel. It continued in use as a private Catholic chapel in the 18th century. The 11th Duke converted it into a dining room *circa* 1795. The mahogany gothic side-tables date from his alterations. The room was enlarged and remodelled by Buckler for the 15th Duke in 1888. The arched ceiling is inspired by that in the old Bishop's Chapel at Mayfield, East Sussex. Characteristic details of Buckler's work are the heraldic tiles made by Mintons in the fireplace and the wrought iron electroliers by Hardman. The full length portraits flanking the main door show the 'Collector Earl' of Arundel as a young man wearing

tilting armour for a Court entertainment of 1610, artist unknown, and Elizabeth, Queen of Bohemia, by Michael Janz Van Mierveldt whose signature can be seen on the edge of the table cloth. The portrait of the 12th Duke in parliamentary robes was painted by Pickersgill to celebrate the passing of the Catholic Emancipation Act in 1829. The quill pen used by George IV to sign the Act is displayed below.

The furniture includes a set of chairs supplied by John Metcalfe for Norfolk House in 1750, all with fine needlework covers dated 1752–62 and worked by Henrietta, Duchess of Gordon, an old relation of the 9th Duke and Duchess who lived with them. The four satinwood pedestal cupboards and urns in neo-classical taste contain trays for hot charcoal and racks to keep the plates warm.

The Boulle clock on the side table by the chimneypiece dates from the early 18th century and was made by Jérôme Martinot; it is surmounted by gilt figures of Minerva and the three Fates controlling the thread of life. Every year the table is laid for breakfast, dinner or dessert with a different selection of family plate, including the 'Grand' and 'Country' dinner services, and the gold and silver dessert services.

Displayed in a glass case are the Earl Marshal's baton, and the gold cups which were presented to the Earl Marshal by sovereigns since George II at their Coronation.

Relics of Mary Queen of Scots

In the case are also displayed some of the greatest treasures at Arundel, the unique assemblage of objects relating to Mary Queen of Scots. The 4th Duke of Norfolk was beheaded by Elizabeth I in 1572 because it was feared that his betrothal to Mary amounted to an attempt on the throne itself. The rosary beads of gold and enamel were carried by Mary at her own execution at Fotheringhay Castle and bequeathed by her to Anne, Countess of Arundel, wife of St Philip Howard. The pomander rosary beads are also 16th-century. The gold cross was bought by Mary Howard (mother of the 8th and 9th Dukes of Norfolk) in 1696 from a Benedictine monk in Paris. It was reputed to have been given by Mary to Abbot Feckenham, the last Abbot of Westminster, who was imprisoned in the Tower from 1560 to 1584. The pearl necklace with gold fleur-de-lys recalls that Mary's first husband was King Francis II of France. This was bought by the 15th Duke from a French nobleman as a wedding present for his wife in 1877. Her prayer book, with 16th-century illuminations, was given to Lord Herries by Mary after the Battle of Langside in 1568 when she sought refuge in his house at Terregles.

Rosary beads of Mary Queen of Scots

THE SMALL DRAWING ROOM

This was redecorated in 1997 with advice from the interior decorator David Mlinaric. The contents came from Norfolk House in London.

The three splendid landscapes by Canaletto were commissioned *circa* 1750 by the 9th Duke and Duchess. They are *cappriccii* – imaginary views, but made up out of parts of real buildings including the porch of St Mark's, Venice. Their frames were made for them by Cuenot. The Louis XV seat furniture (from the Music Room at Norfolk House) is by Jean-Réné Nadal L'Ainé.

The Louis XV marquetry writing table or *bureau plat* with ormolu mounts is by Bernard Van Risenburgh (known as BVRB). The painted neo-classical commode in the Wyatt manner dates from *circa* 1780 and is among the finest pieces of English furniture of its date; the oval panels of classical goddesses, dancers and musicians are after Adam Buck and Angelica Kauffman. On it is a Regency bronze and gilt garniture, the candelabra supported on sphinxes and the little clock on a horse. The Louis XVI ormolu cartel clock, hanging above, is by Joseph Charles Bertrand of Paris, 1772.

THE DRAWING ROOM

The Drawing Room was among Buckler's earliest works for the 15th Duke and dates from 1877. The principal feature is the large heraldic chimney-piece in carved Painswick stone by Thomas Earp with the arms of the 15th Duke impaling those of his first wife Lady Flora Hastings; it cost £150. The carved oak ceiling was made by Rattee & Kett of Cambridge. The painted shields showing the family quarterings from the 13th to the 19th centuries in the cornice were derived from manuscripts at the College of Arms. Buckler, as well as being an architect, was Surrey Herald Extraordinary and worked out the heraldic decorations throughout the Castle from his own researches at the College of Arms.

Some of the 18th-century furniture came from Norfolk House. The matching pier glasses and pier tables, embellished with bunches of grapes, between the windows, were originally in the dining room there. The tables are of ormolu, not gilt wood, and for that reason extremely rare. On them are displayed some early 19th-century miniature copies in enamel by Henry Bone of family portraits. The table at the west end of the room below the Mytens portraits has a particularly good 17th-century Roman *pietra dura* top decorated with agate, jasper and lapis lazuli. On it is a superb Boulle clock with naval symbolism by Claude Artus of *circa* 1690. The two small tables flanking the sofas are an English painted rosewood lady's writing-desk and a Louis XVI kingwood *poudreuse*; on either side of the chimneypiece are gilt Italian neo-classical side tables with marble tops.

The portraits include some of the finest in the Castle. Beginning on the west wall and moving

from left to right they are: Henry Frederick, Earl of Arundel by Van Dyck; the 'Collector Earl' by Daniel Mytens, 1618 (the Earl's sculpture gallery at Arundel House, London, contained the earliest collection of antique marbles in England, now in the Ashmolean Museum at Oxford); Aletheia, Countess of Arundel by Daniel Mytens, 1618 (the garden at Arundel House in the background is the inspiration for the new 'Collector Earl's' Garden at Arundel); William Howard, Viscount Stafford after Van Dyck; Bernard, 12th Duke of Norfolk by Gainsborough; George IV as Prince of Wales by Reynolds; Charles, 11th Duke of Norfolk as a young man by Gainsborough; the 6th Duke of Norfolk and his second wife by Sir Peter Lely; Sir Walter Pye by Van Dyck, and between the pier glasses, Lord Thomas Howard of Worksop by Reynolds.

The room was redecorated in 2006 when the walls were painted moss green and the big sofas made specially by Robert Kime.

Detail from bronze side table c.1750

Louis XIV Boulle clock

THE GRAND STAIRCASE

Opening off the Gallery is the main staircase, a dramatic Victorian composition under a high stone vault. The balustrade decorated with quatrefoils has a handrail of 'fossil marble' and the newels are topped with finely carved heraldic beasts holding shields sporting different quarterings.

On the walls hang two more of the Gobelins tapestries from Norfolk House and a group of portraits of the children of the 13th Duke, including one as a boy of the first Lord Howard of Glossop, the great-great-grandfather of the present Duke.

Underneath the stairs hangs a picture of Worksop Manor in Nottinghamshire by William Hodges, painted in 1770. Worksop was intended to be a palatial principal seat of the Dukes of Norfolk and was designed by James Paine for the 9th Duke, but never finished and demolished after its sale to the Duke of Newcastle in 1838. The English *verre eglomisé* looking-glass with blue and gold borders on the right, dates from the early 18th century and came from Norfolk House. The 18th-century chairs of walnut inlaid with bone are Dutch.

The Portrait of The Earl of Surrey

In the Gallery, facing the bottom of the stairs is a large portrait of Henry Howard, the 'Poet' Earl of Surrey (1517–1547), eldest son of the 3rd Duke of Norfolk, who was beheaded by Henry VIII for quartering the Royal Arms with his own arms, deemed to be a claim to the throne and therefore treason. The supporting figures carry shields to show his royal descent through both his father and mother from Edward I and Edward III respectively. He was a brave soldier and brilliant poet who, together with Thomas Wyatt, was responsible for the introduction of the Italian-sonnet form into England and the creation of blank verse.

THE UPPER GALLERY

At the top of the main staircase a wide passage runs the full width of the south wing above the Picture Gallery. The stonework was cleaned and the whole redecorated in 1994. The paintings include a series of important 15th-century altarpieces acquired by the 15th Duke of Norfolk, notably a Florentine deposition dated 1460 which is by the Master of San Miniato. The Flemish altarpiece of carved and painted wood comes from the Beresford Hope Collection. It was originally made for Ypres Cathedral.

The large nativity scene above the oak stairs is by Benedetto Gennari and was the altarpiece at James II's Catholic Chapel at Whitehall Palace. The two German panels of the Annunciation are dated 1487, and are by Michael Packer. A cheerful contrast is the view of Fairlop Fair in Epping Forest, by C. R. Leslie which was painted for the 12th Duke of Norfolk. The 18th-century oriental lacquer chests and cabinets include several formerly at Worksop Manor. The pair of early 18th-century looking-glasses from Norfolk House have superb red and gold *verre eglomisé* borders (painted on the back of the glass) copied from French engravings.

THE BEDROOMS

THE YORK BEDROOM

This is the principal guest bedroom in the Castle and is called after the York Herald of Arms. Some of the bedrooms at Arundel have been named after heralds since the late 18th century and reflect the fact that the Duke of Norfolk as Earl Marshal is in charge of the College of Arms. The rooms on this floor were restored and redecorated between 1995 and 2002. The hooded stone fireplace was designed by Buckler in mid 13th-century style, and with Minton heraldic tiles. The four-poster bed was made in 1995 incorporating Georgian posts. This room contains three especially fine pieces of furniture: the German marquetry wardrobe dated 1744, the French Louis XVI commode with architectural marquetry and the large rococo looking-glass of *circa* 1750 with Chinese glass paintings, which came from the State Dressing room at Norfolk House. It is partnered by some Chinese Chippendale chairs. The two architectural views were painted by Antonio Joli, Master of Canaletto; they represent Avignon and Messina.

THE YORK DRESSING ROOM

This contains a Victorian bath and wash basin and heated towel rail (still in working order) made in 1890 by Dent and Hellyer of Holborn. These are among a number of similar fittings at Arundel designed by C. A. Buckler for the restored Castle, which at the time was in the forefront of domestic technology. Buckler's large stone fireplace is similar to that in the York Bedroom. For winter house-parties at Arundel log fires are lit in the guest bedrooms and bathrooms.

The York Bedroom

Altarpiece of Passion of Christ, Flemish School (15th century)

BEDROOM NO. 1

This small room intended for a bachelor (only married couples got large bedrooms and dressing rooms) has a Victorian half-tester bed, recently acquired. It is arranged as a Print room with engravings on the walls; these include 26 of Kip and Knyff's bird's-eye views of English country houses, and ten by Wenceslas Hollar (whom the 'Collector' Earl brought from Bohemia to England). The prints were collected and framed by the present Duke of Norfolk's father *circa* 1990.

THE CHESTER BEDROOM

The Chester Bedroom is called after the Chester herald of Arms and was designed by Buckler in the 1870s, in the South Tower. Both walls and ceiling are wainscotted in oak. The mahogany early 19th-century bed was bought in 1987 by the Duke from Callaly Castle, Northumberland. The portraits include the 12th Duke by Mather Brown, the 9th Duke by Reynolds, Queen Victoria by William Fowler and a pair of good early 17th-century portraits on panel by Cornelius Johnson.

THE CHESTER DRESSING ROOM AND BATHROOM

A little flight of stairs leads up to the Chester Dressing Room and bathroom. Here can be seen one of the original Victorian water-closets by Dent and Hellyer. Pictures of Sheffield include photographs of Queen Victoria's Jubilee visit in 1897 and coloured lithographs of the 19th-century city with its picturesque hilly setting and smoking steel works. They recall the family connection with Sheffield where the Norfolk family has had estates since the 17th century, part of the inheritance of Aletheia Talbot, wife of the 'Collector' Earl.

THE LANCASTER BEDROOM

These rooms over the drawing room were remodelled in 1878, and redecorated by the present Duchess under the direction of Edmund Bulmer in 2001–2. The ceiling, painted with leaves from trees in the grounds, is the work of Michael Dillon. The commode with floral marquetry is German 18th-century. The pair of satinwood late 18th-century bookcases were bought by Lavinia Duchess of Norfolk in 1960.

The Chester Bedroom

PORTCULLIS BEDROOM

Portcullis Bedroom is named after Portcullis Pursuivant, one of the four junior officers of arms. The blue and white wallpaper is a reprint of a Watts' Victorian design. The bathroom in the corner turret was inserted in 1938.

THE WINDSOR BEDROOM

This was redecorated in 2002 by Edmund Bulmer re-using a Victorian lavender colour scheme for the walls. The chimneypiece has Minton heraldic tiles designed by C. A. Buckler. The splendid Chippendale four-poster bed was acquired specially for this room by the present Duke and Duchess of Norfolk. The other furniture includes a Dutch oyster marquetry cabinet on stand, and a pair of 18th-century Turin commodes in the manner of Pifetti inlaid with ivory and mother-of-pearl. The silver-framed mirror on the dressing table was a wedding present from the Estate to Duchess Gwendoline in 1904. The two large flower paintings by Jan Baptiste Bosschaert (dated 1706) were originally overdoors at Worksop Manor.

The Windsor Bedroom

THE WINDSOR DRESSING ROOM

The bath and wash basin are Victorian originals supplied by Dent & Hellyer of Holborn *circa* 1890. The late 18th-century Italian commode has marquetry designed by Giuseppe Maggiolini of Milan.

BACK ON THE MAIN FLOOR

THE VICTORIA ROOMS

The outer range of bed and dressing rooms was added to the courtyard side of the Gallery in 1790 as part of the 11th Duke's alterations. A suite of these was refurbished for the visit to Arundel of Queen Victoria and Prince Albert in December 1846. For that occasion the 13th Duke of Norfolk commissioned a complete set of white and gold 'Elizabethan'-style furniture, including a splendid bed from the fashionable decorator George Morant (who had recently carried out much work for the Duchess's parents, the Duke and Duchess of Sutherland, at Stafford House in London).

The portrait of Queen Victoria was also specially commissioned for the occasion and is by William Fowler the Elder.

In the adjoining dressing room are displayed other artefacts connected with Queen Victoria including a pair of steel spades made by a Sheffield tenant for the Queen and the Prince Consort to plant trees in the Castle grounds to commemorate their visit.

The Victoria Bedroom

THE ANTE LIBRARY

This room was redecorated in 2006, the ceiling grained to resemble oak and the walls stencilled in red on a stone-coloured ground in the Victorian 'Norfolk Pattern'. The wrought iron chandelier is modern by a local blacksmith after a design by C. A. Buckler.

This room survives partly as remodelled by the 11th Duke in the early 19th century; the thin ribbed plaster ceiling and moulded plaster cornice date from then. The 15th Duke and his architect Charles Buckler inserted the elaborate chimneypiece during the major rebuilding in 1878.

The heraldry on the fireplace emphasises the early descent of the Dukes of Norfolk. The central shield quarters Howard, Brotherton, Mowbray, Segrave, (Earl) Marshal, Braose, Fitzalan and Warenne. It is flanked to the left by the Norfolk Lion holding a banner of Brotherton and on the right by the Fitzalan Horse holding a banner quartering Fitzalan and Warenne.

The two window alcoves were added to the room in 1898 to improve the natural lighting.

This room holds many fine pieces of furniture, such as the carved ebony cabinet in the recess to the left hand side of the entrance to the Library. It was made in Paris at the workshop of Jean Macé, *circa* 1650.

The four black lacquer cabinets and coffer came from Worksop Manor where, in the 18th century, every dressing room had a piece of lacquer furniture. The set of George I red walnut chairs of *circa* 1730 are covered with original floral needlework.

This room is notable for three magnificent portraits commissioned from Van Dyck by the 14th 'Collector' Earl of Arundel of himself and his family. Flanking the door on the right is the Earl with his grandson 'Little Tom' who was restored as 5th Duke of Norfolk in 1660. It is among the very best of Van Dyck's English portraits, painted 1635–6. To the left of the door is a portrait of Lady Elizabeth Stuart, wife of Henry Frederick, Earl of Arundel; they

French cabinet, 17th century

married on 7 March 1626 without the King's consent, thus forfeiting royal favour. Facing the fireplace is the 'Madagascar' portrait of the Earl and Countess of Arundel, painted in 1639 to commemorate the Earl's unrealised scheme for colonising Madagascar to which he points on the globe.

Over the French ebony cabinet is a portrait of an Italian Nobleman. Bought in the 19th century, it was once attributed to Titian but it is now thought to be by Niccolo dell'Abbate. Flanking the Library door are, on the left, a Van Dyck portrait of an unknown man and, on the right, a Van Dyck portrait of an unknown peeress in widow's clothes. Full length portraits by John Opie of the 10th Duke and Duchess hang in the two window alcoves. She holds a copy of her husband's book: *Anecdotes of the Howard Family*. Looking back, over the Gallery door is a landscape by Gainsborough.

Thomas Howard, 14th Earl of Arundel with his grandson, later 5th Duke of Norfolk, by Van Dyck

THE LIBRARY

The Library is the principal survivor of the 11th Duke's work and is one of the most important Gothic rooms of *circa* 1800 in the country. It is 122 feet (38 metres) long, entirely fitted out in carved Honduras mahogany and treated as if it were a church, with slender clustered columns supporting a ribbed vault. The carved woodwork is by Jonathan Ritson father and son who came from Greystoke in Cumberland and later worked at Petworth. The stone chimneypieces, looking like Perpendicular chantry chapels hollowed out of the thickness of the walls, were inserted by Buckler for the 15th Duke in 1900. The set of mahogany seat furniture, including couches, sofas and arm chairs all upholstered in stamped red velvet, was provided by George Morant for Queen Victoria's visit in 1846. The fitted patterned carpet was supplied at the same time and was rewoven to the original design in 1987 by Grosvenor Woodward. The carved circular table by Morant, in the centre bay, has a top of micro-mosaic made in Rome in 1847 by Michelangelo Barberi for the 13th Duke, whose arms impaled with those of his wife, Charlotte Leveson-Gower, decorate the centre. The pair of Chinese *famille rose* vases date from the early 19th century.

The Library is one of the more important country house collections, rich in manuscript and printed material relating to Catholic history. It comprises ten thousand books and was collected by the 9th and 11th Dukes. The silver icon to the right of the entrance is by Fabergé and was commissioned by the wife of the 15th Duke of Norfolk in 1908. The hanging lanterns are Chinese early 19th century; they were made for a wedding. The celestial globe, *circa* 1770 is by George Adams,

mathematical instrument maker to George III. The terrestrial globe was made to match in the early 19th century. The 16th-century painted Italian Pageant Shield was acquired by the 'Collector' Earl of Arundel in the early 17th century and is one of the few objects remaining from his great art collection. It is painted on both sides in gold and grisaille with scenes from Roman history, and is thought to be one of a set made for the entry into Milan of Charles V as Emperor. (Others are in New York and Philadelphia.)

Above: Silver icon by Fabergé

Above: Pageant Shield c.1538 – made for the entry of Charles V into Milan

Below: Antwerp Cabinet 17th century

THE SOUTH PASSAGE

The chief architectural interest of this long passage is that the south (left-hand) wall was the original 1180 courtyard-frontage of the South Bailey. One of the original buttresses, two of the double splayed windows and a round arched doorway survive in good condition. The latter gives access to the medieval undercroft which has a barrel vault of chalk. The other rooms opening off this passage are all domestic offices including the butler's pantry, still room and china cupboard. The Victorian kitchen at the west end is now the Castle shop. The passage is lined with stags' heads from the herd of red deer kept in the park from 1790 to 1939. The eagle owls were introduced by the 11th Duke and lived in the Keep till the ivy was taken off in the 1860s. They are named after statesmen incuding Lord Thurlow (a Lord Chancellor in the time of George III). The pole arms and breast plates are the Arundel 'second eleven'. The 'medieval' helmets are outright fakes by Grimshaw, a Victorian forger.

THE FRONT HALL

This was called the Guard Room by the antiquarian-minded Buckler and has a stone ribbed vault copied from New College, Oxford. The early 18th-century hall chairs have always been at Arundel. The seven Greek altars are survivors from the 'Collector' Earl's ancient marbles (now mainly in the Ashmolean Museum at Oxford). The statue by John Francis is of Lady Adeliza Fitzalan Howard, the younger daughter of the 13th Duke. The hooded leather Porter's Chair comes from Norfolk House. Opposite the central arches is the 16th-century overmantel from the old Admiralty Office at Deptford. It has the 3rd Duke's arms as Lord High Admiral. Nearby in a glass case is a model of the 15th Duke's yacht 'Star of the Sea', made at Leith in 1878.

Statue of Lady Adeliza Fitzalan Howard by John Francis

Overmantel from the old Admiralty Office

Model of 'Star of the Sea'

Hooded leather Porter's Chair

THE FITZALAN CHAPEL

The Fitzalan Chapel was founded in 1380 by Richard, 4th Earl of Arundel in accordance with his father's intention, as a collegiate chapel served by secular priests. In the later Middle Ages it was a notable centre of music with a fine choir for which much early English polyphony was specially composed. In the reign of Henry VIII the college was dissolved; the chapel and other buildings were returned to the family and have been the private property of the Earls of Arundel and the Dukes of Norfolk ever since. In 1879 an action heard before Lord Chief Justice Coleridge determined that the Fitzalan Chapel did not form part of the parish church but was an independent ecclesiastical structure. The chapel has therefore remained Catholic, an unusual, if not unique, anomaly in England though such arrangements are more common in Germany.

The chapel was damaged in the Civil War in 1643–4, and during the following century and a half suffered more from neglect, culminating in the destruction of the original carved timber roof in 1782. The building was restored in stages in the course of the 19th century. *Circa* 1837 the 12th Duke of Norfolk carried out various repairs under the direction of Robert Abraham, including the renewal of the windows. The 14th Duke added the mausoleum on the south side to the design of M. E. Hadfield. A major restoration was undertaken by the 15th Duke in 1886 to the plans of C. A. Buckler. The wood carving was executed by Messrs Rattee and Kett of Cambridge. Every piece of old fabric which could be saved was re-used and the new work was a careful reconstruction of the original.

The chapel is still used as the burial place of the Dukes of Norfolk and several masses are said here every year for the repose of their souls in accordance with the intention of the founder in the 14th century. The major artistic interest of the Fitzalan Chapel lies in the tombs of the Earls of Arundel and Dukes of Norfolk which form one of the finest assemblages of their kind in England. (A separate guide-leaflet describing these is available.)

Roundheads encamped in the Fitzalan Chapel by Joseph Nash 1860

THE GARDENS

THE GARDENS

The grounds at Arundel cover over 30 acres and include features dating from many centuries, though they owe much of their present appearance to the work of the present Duchess of Norfolk over the last twenty years. She has carried out extensive new planting and created several new gardens. The Little Park (now the cricket ground) to the north, the fish ponds to the east and the bowling green (now Rose Garden) to the south of the Castle are all medieval, but the town in those days came right up to the western ditch of the Castle and the Marygate was originally the Town Gate.

The 8th Duke in the early 18th century landscaped the immediate surroundings, planting trees, laying out walks along the earthworks and converting the North Bailey into a vegetable garden. The 11th Duke in 1790 diverted the London road to the other side of the churchyard, so that the old line became a private drive lined with Ilex trees. He established the walled kitchen garden on the present site. It was much enlarged in the mid 19th century when a series of iron-framed greenhouses was erected, of which the Vinery still survives. The High Street Lodge was built to the design of William Burn at the same time and is dated 1850. The 15th Duke completed the basic layout in the 1890s when he created the new Mill Road, built the Lower Lodge (Visitor Entrance) and laid out the drive by which visitors approach the Castle.

THE LOWER LAWNS

The Lower Lawns date from the 15th Duke's time and have recently been planted with Indian Bean trees and banks of shrubs. The visitor has a good view of the South Front from this area which is used for concerts and other events.

THE ROSE GARDEN

The Rose Garden occupies the site of a medieval bowling green. It is enclosed by yew hedges and laid out with formal beds of Rosa Rugosa Alba, Rosa Winchester Cathedral, Rosa Alfred Carrière and Rosa Isaac Perrière. The sun dial is by Jeremiah and Walter Watkins, Charing Cross, London and dated 1785. The carved stone base is by Joseph Teasdale, the 11th Duke's master mason.

The Fitzalan Chapel Garden

THE FITZALAN CHAPEL GARDEN

The Fitzalan Chapel Garden is an attractive, small enclosure which is planted as a knot garden with four beds round a small pond. It has a white theme, planted in summer with Penstemens, tender perennials and annuals, giving it a peaceful atmosphere before entering the chapel. Four palm trees flourish in this sheltered space.

THE WALLED GARDEN

The Walled Garden, behind the parish church, was constructed in the 19th century. The wrought iron gates were a wedding present to the 16th Duke and his wife from his mother in 1937. There are good views of the Catholic Cathedral built by the 15th Duke to the design of J. A. Hansom in 1868–73.

THE 'COLLECTOR' EARL'S GARDEN

The 'Collector' Earl's Garden was opened by the Prince of Wales in 2008. This new formal garden is a light-hearted tribute to Thomas Howard, 14th

Oberon's Palace

Below left: The Park Temple

Earl of Arundel (1585–1646), known as 'The Collector'. It has been designed by Isabel and Julian Bannerman with Russell Taylor as job architect, and has been conceived as a Jacobean formal garden (*see the previous pages*). It is in fact an imaginative recreation of what the 'Collector' Earl's formal garden may have been like at Arundel House, his town palace overlooking the Thames in London. The domed pergola and fountains are based on those seen in the garden vista in the background of the famous Mytens portrait of the Countess of Arundel (in the drawing room here), while the various gateways and pavilions are based on Inigo Jones's designs for Arundel House. They have been executed in green oak and have a rustic charm and robust character appropriate to the garden.

The grand centrepiece is the rockwork 'mountain' planted with palms and unusual ferns to represent another world, supporting a green oak version of 'Oberon's Palace', a fantastic spectacle designed by Inigo Jones for Prince Henry's Masque on New Year's Day 1611, flanked by two green oak obelisks. This contains a shell-lined interior with a stalagmite fountain and gilded coronet 'dancing' on a jet of water.

The garden is divided into formal courts with a centre canal pond and tufa-lined cascade. The planting is restrained – no flowers but scented magnolia grandiflora, Indian Bean Trees, shrubs and semi-tropical plants taking advantage of the walls to trap heat.

The 'Dancing Coronet' in Oberon's Palace

THE CUTTING GARDEN

The central section has herbaceous borders backed by yew hedges and the large bed is planted with flowers for the house, including a collection of perennials: Penstemens, Salvias, Cannas and Dahlias in season.

The principal feature in the central garden is the iron-framed Victorian Greenhouse. It was built as a vinery and is the survivor from a pair of metal-framed hot houses supplied in 1850 by the firm Jones & Clark, later Clark & Hope of Birmingham (who also supplied greenhouses for the Royal Gardens at Osborne and Frogmore, Windsor in 1849). The firm was founded in 1818 and provided hot houses for many country houses, and were asked to submit designs for the new Palm House at Kew. Clark & Hope were the leading Victorian manufacturers of metal-framed greenhouses. The

The Gardens

The Flower Gardens

The Vinery and Peach House

Arundel Vinery is a good survival of their work. It is a traditional lean-to design, the frame being made of wrought iron. It was restored and replanted in 1995. The new vines, and also the peaches and nectarines, are the same varieties as those originally grown (recorded in the Victorian garden accounts in the Castle archives).

THE KITCHEN GARDEN

The Kitchen Garden has been restored as a Victorian kitchen garden growing vegetables and fruits using organic methods. The garden is divided into box-edged beds with different vegetables in each and uses companion planting of flowers to encourage bees and other beneficial insects as well as looking decorative. It is not just for display as the produce is used to supply the castle. Down the centre is a pergola of espaliered apple trees. The new wooden framed greenhouse of traditional design, grows plants for the house and unusual vegetables. One section grows melons, gourds and chillies; the other, tropical plants such as pineapples, papaya, bananas and passion fruit.

THE MARYGATE

The Marygate adjoins the walled garden, and now forms the private entrance from the park. This was the medieval town gate of Arundel; though restored, it dates from *circa* 1295.

THE AMERICAN GROUND

The area between the Castle and the walled garden was known in the 19th century as the American Ground and was planted with imported and exotic trees and shrubs. There remains a fine cork oak and several holm, or evergreen oaks. The banks are planted with Narcissus species for spring interest, and small trees with good autumn colour: *Prunus Sargenti, Parotia Persica, Ruonymus Arbutus.* The grass is left long in areas to preserve rare species of orchid (Bee Orchid) and other natural flora.

106

In Stoke Church iuxta Neyland Com. Suffolk

n the East window of the South part in the saide Church are these portratures of Sr Iohn Howard knight, and Dame Alice his wife, daughter and heire of Sr William Tendring knight, wth this subscription.

rate pro aniābus Domini Johannis Howard, et Dominæ Aliciæ vroris eius.

THE FITZALAN HOWARD FAMILY

Arundel has passed by descent (with small interruptions and twice through female heiresses) from 1138, when it was granted to Queen Adeliza and her husband William de Albini, to the present Duke of Norfolk.

In 1243 on the death of William's descendant Hugh 'in the flower of his youth', John Fitzalan, feudal lord of Clun and Oswaldestre, inherited the Castle and Honour of Arundel through his mother Isabel d'Aubigny or de Albini. His grandson Richard was created Earl of Arundel. The Fitzalans were Earls of Arundel and held the Castle until 1580 and the death of the 12th Earl. His daughter Mary married Thomas, 4th Duke of Norfolk in 1556 and their only son Philip inherited the Earldom and the Castle, thus uniting the Fitzalans and the Howards. The Fitzalans for centuries played their part among the highest nobility of England. Indeed, in the 15th century following a challenge from the Earls of Devon, the Earldom of Arundel was established 'in its original supremacy of honour above every other similar title of dignity'. Successive Earls fought for the King in Wales, Scotland and France, were prominent in public life, and were patrons of literature and music including the printer Caxton and the composer Tallis.

Richard Fitzalan, created Earl of Arundel in 1290, fought for Edward I at the siege of Caerlaverock and is commemorated in a ballad. His son Edmund was caught up in the bloody intrigues of Edward II's reign and was beheaded at Hereford in 1326 by Queen Isabella's lover, Mortimer. Arundel Castle was seized and granted to the Earl of Kent (6th son of Edward I) who was in turn beheaded in 1330, and the following year the Fitzalans were restored to their estates and title in the person of Edmund's son, Richard. He later succeeded to the enormous possessions of the Warenne family on the death of his mother's brother, the Earl of Surrey. This Richard, 3rd Earl of Arundel, commanded the second division at Crecy and was the richest man in England. His son Richard, 4th Earl, was a close associate of Edward III in the French Wars and carried the crown at the coronation of Richard II, but later turned against the King and, though pardoned, was treacherously arrested, tried at Westminster and executed, 'no more shrinking' from his fate 'or changing colour than if he were going to a banquet'. He built the Parish Church of St Nicholas at Arundel combined with The Collegiate Chapel of the Holy Trinity, now called the Fitzalan Chapel.

For a short interval Arundel was granted by Richard II to John Holland, Duke of Exeter, but on the accession of Henry IV Thomas Fitzalan was restored in blood and made a Knight of the Garter. He married Beatrice, daughter of King John I of Portugal and later played an active part under Henry V in campaigns against the Welsh and French. He died of dysentery at the siege of Harfleur in 1415 just before Agincourt. His superb alabaster tomb with effigies of himself and Beatrice of Portugal is the centrepiece of the Fitzalan Chapel. The next three Earls of Arundel were cousins of Thomas, they too were soldiers. The 7th Earl, John, was made a Knight of the Bath and Lord Maltravers by Henry VI in 1426 and Duke of Touraine in France by the Regent Duke of Bedford. He died aged twenty-seven following the amputation of a leg at Beauvais in 1435. Because of his military prowess he was known as the 'English Achilles'. His tomb on the north side of the Fitzalan Chapel shows him resplendent in tabard and full armour while underneath lies a cadaver. John's infant son died at the age of ten so the Earldom passed to an uncle, William, a Yorkist supporter. He too was made a Knight of the Garter, Governor of Dover Castle and Warden of the Cinque Ports. He married Lady Joan Neville, sister of Warwick 'the King Maker'. Their gothic chantry of Purbeck marble with fine Caen stone effigies on the south side of the Fitzalan Chapel is among the finest of its period. The last Earls of Arundel of the Fitzalan line were all prominent courtiers and soldiers. William, 11th Earl, was a close friend of Henry VIII and supported the King in his attempt to divorce Catherine of Aragon. Henry, 12th Earl, was a godson of Henry VIII, a Knight of the Garter, Deputy Governor of Calais and a distinguished participant in

Henry Howard, the 'Poet' Earl of Surrey 1517–1547
Courtesy of the National Portrait Gallery

the Siege of Boulogne in 1544. He also formed a large library later bought by James I and now part of the British Library. On his death in 1580 his honours and the Castle passed to his grandson, Saint Philip Howard, 13th Earl of Arundel and the eldest son of the 4th Duke of Norfolk.

THE HOWARDS, DUKES OF NORFOLK

In 1483 John, Lord Howard had been created Duke of Norfolk, Marshal and Earl Marshal of England by King Richard III. He was also Lord Admiral of England, Ireland and Aquitaine and Deputy Governor of Calais. He came of a long line of distinguished Norfolk gentry, whose first notable ancestor was Sir William Howard, a judge of the Court of Common Pleas in the reign of Edward I. His mother was Lady Margaret Mowbray, daughter of Thomas Mowbray, Duke of Norfolk, and a descendant of Edward I. John, 1st (Howard) Duke of Norfolk was a loyal supporter of Richard III and coheir to the Mowbray estates. He was killed at the Battle of Bosworth in 1485. Thomas, 2nd Duke of Norfolk, commanded the vanguard under his father at Bosworth Field where he was wounded, taken prisoner by Henry VII and lost the Dukedom by attainder. He spent three years in the Tower of London and was eventually released after swearing allegiance to Henry VII. Known as the Earl of Surrey, he was a brilliant military commander and his greatest achievement was, when aged 70, he commanded the victorious English Army against the Scots at Flodden in 1513. His reward was the restoration of the Dukedom and he was allowed to add to his arms the Honorary Augmentation of an escutcheon 'charged with a demi-lion rampant pierced through the mouth by an arrow'. He died aged 80 in 1524 and his ceremonial funeral with processions across East Anglia lasted four weeks. His son, Thomas, 3rd Duke, was the model of the self-seeking Tudor courtier determined to survive amidst the deadly politics of Henry VIII's Court. Responsible for two Queens of England, the importance of the 3rd Duke cannot be over-estimated. The most notorious of the Dukes of Norfolk, he was prepared to sacrifice his family to retain the favour of Henry VIII. He managed to bring his two attractive nieces to Court and subsequently to the attentions of the King. The first, Anne Boleyn, became the second wife of Henry VIII and mother of Elizabeth I. Later, the second niece, Katherine Howard, married Henry as his fifth wife. Both perished on the block.

His own daughter, Mary, he married to Henry's illegitimate son, Henry Fitzroy, Duke of Richmond, but the boy died aged seventeen years, leaving the marriage unconsummated, so in this manoeuvre too his cunning plans were thwarted. Though the leader of the Catholic party in England and a friend of Saint Thomas More, he was nevertheless principally responsible for the bloody suppression of the 'Pilgrimage of Grace'. Despite his political acumen he fell victim to the rival faction of the Protestant Duke of Somerset at the end of Henry's reign. His son, the 'Poet' Earl of Surrey, 'excellent in arts and in arms, a man of learning, a genius and a hero', famous for his sonnets and the creation of blank verse, was executed on a charge of quartering the arms of Edward the Confessor, tantamount in heraldic terms to a claim to the throne. The Duke himself only escaped the death penalty because Henry VIII died the day before sentence was due to be carried out

The Earl of Surrey defending his former allegiance to Richard III before Henry VII, by Mather Brown, 1797

and it was not wished to begin the new reign with bloodshed. He spent the reign of Edward VI in the Tower, but was restored by Queen Mary, dying against the odds in his bed at the age of 80.

The accession of Thomas, 4th Duke, saw a further family tragedy. He lacked his grandfather's sure political sense and was beheaded by order of Queen Elizabeth I on Tower Hill in 1572 at the age of 34 for plotting to marry Mary Queen of Scots (Catholic heir to the throne) as his fourth wife. The Dukedom was attainted, but his son, Philip inherited his mother's family title as 13th Earl of Arundel, and her estates including Arundel Castle.

He enthusiastically embraced the Faith of his ancestors at a time when Anglicanism had finally become the established religion in England. He tried to leave the country without Queen Elizabeth's permission but was captured, and imprisoned in the Tower where he died of dysentery ten years later. Over the chimneypiece in his cell he wrote in Latin: 'The more affliction for Christ in this world, so much the more glory with Christ in the future', which can still be read. He was canonised by Pope Paul VI in 1970 and his remains are now enshrined in Arundel Cathedral.

THE 'COLLECTOR' EARL AND CIVIL WAR

The former lustre of the Howards was partly recovered in the person of Thomas, 14th Earl of Arundel. He was restored to many of the family honours, but not the Dukedom, and was created Earl Marshal. He filled several official positions; for instance, he was Ambassador from Charles I to the Emperor in 1633–36 on behalf of the King's sister Elizabeth, the Winter Queen, widow of the Count Palatine of the Rhine. He married Aletheia Talbot, daughter and heiress of the 7th Earl of Shrewsbury, and used her fortune to build up the greatest

The 'Collector' Earl – Thomas Howard, 14th Earl of Arundel by Sir Anthony Van Dyke

aristocratic collection in England and to encourage the arts and learning. He was a patron of Inigo Jones, Rubens and Van Dyck. His collection of ancient marble statues was the first of its kind in northern Europe and is now mainly in the Ashmolean Museum, Oxford. His splendid library was given to the Royal Society by his grandson. He left England on the outbreak of Civil War in 1642 and never returned, dying at Padua in 1646.

The 'Collector' Earl's grandson, Thomas, 16th Earl of Arundel, was restored as 5th Duke of Norfolk by Charles II in 1660, but spent all his life in Italy after becoming ill while studying at Padua University. The 6th Duke, his younger brother, travelled widely visiting India and North Africa, and was a Founder Member of the Royal Society. He was created Hereditary Earl Marshal by Charles II. His public life, however, was curtailed by his Catholicism. Perhaps the most distinguished member of the family in the late 17th century was Philip Howard, a younger brother, who became a Dominican friar and Lord Almoner to Catherine of Braganza, consort of Charles II. He later became a cardinal in Rome.

The 7th Duke, by contrast, conformed to the Established Church, and supported William III in 1688. He divorced his wife and had no children. His nephew the 8th Duke was a strong Catholic. He considered building a new house at Arundel to the design of James Gibbs, but this was never executed and he lived at Worksop Manor in Nottinghamshire instead. His brother Edward, 9th Duke, married the beautiful Mary Blount, a woman of character and taste. Together they built and furnished Norfolk House in London and rebuilt Worksop Manor as well as carrying out repairs to Arundel, but their nephew and heir died young and Worksop was never completed. The 9th Duke lived to be 90, so far a record for a Duke of Norfolk!

On his death in 1777 the Dukedom passed to a kinsman, Charles Howard of Greystoke in Cumberland. His son, also Charles, the 11th Duke, was a personal friend of the Prince Regent, later George IV, a keen Foxite, chairman of the Whig Club and an amateur architect. He began the reconstruction of the Castle, and made the Park, and erected Hiorne's Tower to the design of Francis Hiorne of Warwick. He also modernised the estates, and collected the finest books in the library, but is – perhaps unfairly – best remembered for his heavy drinking habits and a dozen illegitimate children.

THE VICTORIAN AND MODERN DUKES

The 11th Duke died in 1815 and was succeeded by a cousin, Bernard, 12th Duke, who in 1824 was permitted to exercise the office of Earl Marshal, although a Catholic, and in 1829 was allowed to take his seat in the House of Lords after the Catholic Emancipation Act. Henry, 13th Duke, was Master of the Horse as well as Earl Marshal. He entertained Queen Victoria at Arundel in 1846. Henry Granville, 14th Duke, was educated at Cambridge and served in the Life Guards. He was an active Catholic theorist, the author of *A Few Remarks on the Social and Political Conditions of the British Catholics*. He was a friend of many leading Catholic figures including Pugin, Ambrose Phillips de Lisle and Newman. He started to reconstruct the Castle to the design of M. E. Hadfield but died before work was completed and his son

Henry Granville Fitzalan Howard, 14th Duke of Norfolk, with Augusta Minna Lyons and their three elder children by Victor Dartiguenave 1845

Henry, 15th Duke, turned instead to C. A. Buckler. Together they restored and reconstructed the whole castle between 1875 and 1900. The 15th Duke played a leading part in late 19th-century Catholic affairs and was also Postmaster General in Lord Salisbury's government from 1895–1900. He died in 1917 and was succeeded by his son Bernard Marmaduke, 16th Duke of Norfolk, who was a well-known public figure in his role as Earl Marshal at the State Funerals of George V, George VI and Winston Churchill, the coronations of George VI and Queen Elizabeth II and the investiture of Prince Charles as Prince of Wales.

Duke Bernard held many public positions. He was President of the MCC and Manager of the English cricket team during the 1962–63 tour of Australia and New Zealand. He was a Senior Steward of the Jockey Club and Her Majesty's Representative at Ascot for 27 years. In 1974 he won the Ascot Gold Cup with Ragstone which he had bred and trained.

Duke Bernard died in 1975, leaving a widow Lavinia and four daughters, the eldest of whom succeeded as the Baroness Herries. Lavinia, Duchess of Norfolk was appointed Lord-Lieutenant of West Sussex (1975–1990), the first woman to hold such office and in 1990 she was installed as the first non-Royal Lady Companion of the Order of the Garter. She died in 1995.

The Dukedom and all the other titles passed in 1975 to a kinsman, Major-General Miles Francis Stapleton Fitzalan Howard, 12th Lord Beaumont and 4th Lord Howard of Glossop. The 17th Duke of Norfolk died in 2002. He had a distinguished military career, serving in the Army for 30 years. He was Head of the British Military Mission to Russian Forces in Germany in 1957–59. He commanded 70 Brigade of the King's African Rifles just before the independence of Kenya in 1963 and later was GOC First Division in Rhine Army 1963–65. He married Anne Mary Constable-Maxwell, a great-grand-daughter of the 10th Lord Herries and a descendent of Saint Thomas More. They had two sons and three daughters. The eldest son, Edward is now 18th Duke of Norfolk. He married Georgina Gore in 1987 and they soon after moved back into the Castle. The present Duke and Duchess have five children, three sons and two daughters, the eldest being Henry Arundel who is studying Economics at Bristol University and is a keen racing driver currently competing in International Formula 3.

The Duke is hereditary Earl Marshal of England in which role he supervises the College of Arms, organises the State Opening of Parliament each year and takes part in other ceremonial occasions. He read Politics, Philosophy and Economics at Oxford and now manages the family estates and other businesses in Sussex, Norfolk and Yorkshire. He and the Duchess have restored Arundel Castle, and laid out the new gardens over the last 20 years.

THE DUKES OF NORFOLK

JOHN
1st Duke of Norfolk

THOMAS
2nd Duke of Norfolk

THOMAS
3rd Duke of Norfolk

THOMAS
4th Duke of Norfolk

THOMAS, as a boy
5th Duke of Norfolk

HENRY
6th Duke of Norfolk

HENRY
7th Duke of Norfolk

THOMAS
8th Duke of Norfolk

EDWARD
9th Duke of Norfolk

CHARLES
10th Duke of Norfolk

CHARLES
11th Duke of Norfolk

BERNARD
12th Duke of Norfolk

HENRY CHARLES
13th Duke of Norfolk

HENRY GRANVILLE
14th Duke of Norfolk

HENRY
15th Duke of Norfolk

BERNARD MARMADUKE
16th Duke of Norfolk

MILES FRANCIS
17th Duke of Norfolk

EDWARD
18th Duke of Norfolk